Bohemia

Heaven's Forge

*A true life account
of
Jan Hus & Jan Zizka*

written & illustrated by
Jerry and Faith McCollough

Copyright © 2021 Jerry and Faith McCollough
All rights reserved. No part of this publication may be reproduced, stored in a retrieval system, or transmitted in any form or by any means electronic, mechanical, photocopying, recording, or otherwise without the prior written permission of the publisher and copyright owners.

ISBN 978-1-953935-10-6
Library of Congress Control Number: 2021938450

Acknowledgements:
James and Sherry Sabella
Helena Polivkova
Kim Knapp
Obie Harrup III
Jonathan Scroggins
Bruce Braithwaite

Editing: Joyce Booze
Typesetting and prepress: Faith McCollough
Production: Jerry and Faith McCollough

Printed in the USA
Published by Tell The Kids, LLC
Fort Worth, TX

TellTheKids.com

Part One

JAN HUS
Flame of Truth

The story begins somewhere in the Czech Republic.

In the early 1400s the people of Europe were oppressed by a corrupt church hierarchy based in Rome. There were stirrings within the priesthood about returning to the original Scriptures, but with kings and princes intimidated by threats from the Church, who would dare raise a voice in opposition? Who would have the courage to confront this evil and bring the truth of the Bible to the nations?

In Bohemia - the present Czech Republic - a single voice was raised. Jan Hus boldly spoke out to challenge those within the Church who had strayed from Jesus' example of what Christians should be. His words stirred people's hearts, and the one-eyed Bohemian general, Jan Zizka, stepped forward to be the champion who would lead them in the ultimate deliverance of all Europe from this oppression.

Jan wanted to have a better life when he grew up. He hoped to become a priest so that he would have a nice robe and enough to eat. In those days, anyone who wanted to become a priest, monk or nun had to be either wealthy enough to buy the position from the archbishop, or be a good enough scholar to be sponsored by some wealthy person. Since Jan had no money, he chose to study hard and learn to be a good scholar.

Do people now pay to become priests and nuns?

Oh, no. Many changes happened because of what Jan Hus started, and people today become pastors, priests and nuns because God speaks to their hearts and asks them to commit their lives to Him. Many of the clergy in Jan Hus' time bought their positions in order to use their power to gain riches for themselves. Jan came to feel that was wrong. The more he read of the Bible, the more strongly he became convinced that buying a position in the church was not pleasing to God.

Do you mean that he didn't feel that way in the beginning?

No. When he was a young man at university he wore fine clothes. His robes had hoods lined with white fur. When he learned how to read the Bible, his ideas changed.

Most Bibles were written in Latin, so only the priests were able to read them. Since Jan wanted to be a priest, he did everything he could to get an education. When he was 13, he entered the school at Prachatice, not far from Husinec, where he studied grammar, rhetoric and logic in preparation for learning Latin. He supported himself as a singer in one of the churches.

From Prachatice he went to Prague where, in 1390 when he was 18, he went to the University to continue his studies. He must have been either very smart or have studied very hard, since he was one of the few students from Prachatice who was able to qualify for the university level. In Prague he shortened his name to Hus and supported himself as a choir boy. It was a time of hunger and want for him, and he said, "I used to make a spoon out of bread to eat peas with until I had consumed the spoon as well." He learned Latin, and after three years graduated with a Bachelor's Degree, then went on to earn his Master's Degree. During this time he also learned German.

After learning to read the Bible, he said, "Woe is me! How many times I have transgressed the Holy Word, rising and doffing my hood or bowing to a rich man but not a poor one, and sending money to the rich man to buy drinks but giving nothing to the poor! I trust, however, our merciful Jesus, our Savior, that He will forgive me and preserve me henceforth from such conduct."

"But why did Jan's reading the Bible make him feel differently from the other priests?"

"Because many of his Czech teachers had studied the philosophy of the English priest, John Wyclif, whose writings had begun to arrive in Bohemia. Wyclif felt that the church ought to return to the way it was when it started, as described in the New Testament."

"How was it different then?"

"The followers of Jesus' teachings practiced a simple lifestyle, owned very little and devoted their lives to helping the people around them. This was the way they had lived when Jesus was with them. In Hus' time the bishops, priests, monks and nuns felt that the church should represent Christ as king since by Jesus' death on the cross He had defeated Satan and was now king over all and ruler of the universe. As representatives of Christ as king, they owned estates and lands, wore expensive robes and jewelry, and lived in comfort while the common people lived in poverty."

"But if God is ruler of everything, were they wrong?"

Wyclif seemed to think so, and after a while so did Jan Hus, since the Bible teaches that when Jesus comes a second time, He will rule and reign as King over the whole earth. Hus objected most strongly to the immoral lifestyle that many of the clergy lived. They spent much of their time drinking, gambling, and committing adultery. They required payment to intercede before God on behalf of people. Hus called Prague's wealthiest clergy, "The Lord's fat ones" because they became wealthy by charging high fees for administering sacraments. They also took multiple paid positions without serving faithfully in any. While claiming that they had inherited the apostles' authority, their lifestyle bore no resemblance to the apostles' way of living.

Jan found that many before him had reached the same conclusions he had. They all believed that living a selfish, dishonest, and immoral lifestyle was inconsistent with what Jesus taught. He was influenced by such men as Stanislav of Znojmo, Stephen of Palec, Matthew of Janov, and Charles Waldhausen in addition to Wyclif. None of them changed history in the same way Jan Hus did, because he openly proclaimed his beliefs before the people. That led to a national uprising.

Jan became a teacher at the university in 1396. He hand-copied the works of Wyclif. He found that Wyclif had been influenced by such men as St. Augustine, Bishop Grosseteste, Archbishop Bradwardine and William of Ockham. Jan didn't agree with all that Wyclif taught, but he did agree that it was important for the clergy to practice the morality of the Bible in their personal lives.

Within 6 years of graduation from university, Jan was appointed the pastor of Bethlehem Chapel, an important church in Prague. From this pulpit he was able to present the message of the Bible clearly, preaching in the Czech language instead of Latin, so that everyone could understand his message. He felt that in an age when printed books were not available, it was important to stress "the living voice of the Gospel".

Bethlehem Chapel was the only church in Prague where the Czech language was used in preaching so that the common people could understand. On the walls were unusual paintings depicting contrasting scenes from which the viewer might conclude that the pope was the Antichrist and that the Roman church was the Antichrist's heretical sect. One picture showed the pope astride a horse, resplendent in all his pomp, while next to it was a picture of Christ in all His poverty, carrying a cross. Another showed the two emperors placing a golden crown on the pope's head, while he wore a purple mantle. They were holding the stirrup, helping him into the saddle. Next to this picture was one of Christ before Pilate, with a crown of thorns being placed on His head. Another showed people kissing the pope's feet, while next to it was one showing Christ washing His disciples' feet.

Jan wasn't against the Roman church, but he felt that many of the clergy weren't living according to what the Bible taught. Jan Hus taught that everyone, including the clergy, should live an honest, moral lifestyle. In fact, the clergy should set the example for everyone else. This made many of the other priests and bishops angry, because they liked the money they received from renting church-owned lands, and from the fees they charged for prayers, sacraments and indulgences.

The church taught that after death, a person's soul had to spend a certain amount of time in purgatory before being allowed into heaven. This time could be shortened by prayers of other believers after the person died. It could also be shortened by the person receiving an "indulgence" from the church while he or she was still living. So, by paying money to the priest anyone could be promised a shorter time in purgatory.

Wyclif not only disagreed with the selling of God's favor, he asserted that the Bible doesn't teach that a believer has to spend time in purgatory before going to heaven. Jan Hus may not have agreed entirely with Wyclif on this point, but he did take a strong stand against the selling of indulgences when the pope began to aggressively push their sale to finance a war against a Christian king, Ladislas of Naples. King Wenceslas of Bohemia would receive some of the profits from the sales, so he prohibited any preaching against indulgences.

Jan began an active campaign against this act, which he felt was a gross misuse of the papal office. He confronted King Wenceslas and said, "No one is truly the Vicar of Christ unless he follow Him in very way of life." In Bethlehem Chapel, Hus preached, "Will you stand with me? Then gird on your swords and prepare for battle." He was speaking figuratively, but the people took him literally, and decided to take the battle to the streets. They began a huge march on the town hall to protest the sale of indulgences. Three young men, Hus' students, were arrested. King Wenceslas assured Hus that they would be safe; then he had them executed in the town square as an example to those who might oppose the sale of indulgences! This inflamed the passions of Hus' followers and marked the beginning of the revolution which was follow.

This is not what Jan wanted. Others such as Jerome of Prague and Nicholas of Dresden stirred the crowds up. Jerome had studied at Oxford University in England, and he had copied several of Wyclif's works while there. He was an outspoken proponent of Wyclif's philosophies. In fact, he was more outspoken than Jan Hus. Nicholas used a more visual approach, making picture placards showing the pope acting the opposite of what Jesus would do.

When word of the crowd's reaction to Jan's sermon reached the pope, he excommunicated Jan. Jan went into exile in an outlying village

Do you mean that Jan was no longer a priest?

Well, that's what the Roman church wanted, but officials in Bohemia came to Jan's defense. Dr. Jan Jesenic, an attorney, presented a defense before the university masters to prove the excommunication false. He argued that the pope was living in mortal sin, and excommunication by anyone in mortal sin is not valid. Wenceslas and his officials agreed to support Jan Hus in order to bring unity in the Bohemian church. Aware that there could be no agreement with Rome, Jan remained in exile, where he spent his time writing over 15 books. To the continued uncertainty of his right to priesthood, Jan responded, "I have preached in towns and market places; now I preach behind hedges, in villages, castles, fields, woods. If it were possible, I would preach on the seashore, or from a ship as my Savior did."

The stand Hus took on excommunication was, "It is impossible to excommunicate a man justly, unless he first excommmunicates himself by sinning mortally." He felt that he should suffer it humbly and rejoice that he has been deemed worthy to suffer for righteousness' sake. He also felt that an ecclesiastical superior who sins may be reprimanded by his inferior, even a layman, although with respect. He emphasized the moral character of the priestly office rather than the ceremonial.

In Prague and surrounding towns violence broke out in the streets with the crowds attacking the clergy whom they felt were abusing their offices. Jan avoided the violence, concentrating instead on writing papers presenting his point of view on the practices of the church. His writing became more and more like Wyclif's, especially on the basic nature of the church

Hus' approach to the civil disobedience taking place in the streets was to write about the relationship between church and state, based on his interpretation of Scripture. He felt that King Wenceslas should have authority over the churches within his realm, rather than all power resting with the pope in Rome. His reasoning was based on how the Lord's Supper was interpreted. Was authority given to the church or to the people? If to the people, then secular rulers should prevail. He wrote, "O what madness to condemn as erroneous the Gospel of Christ, the Epistle of Paul, which he said he received not from man, but from Christ, and the acts of the apostles and other saints. To condemn, that is, communion with the Lord's cup, instituted for all faithful adults. See how they call it error, namely to permit the laity to drink of the Lord's chalice. O St. Paul!...now it is said that the custom of the Roman church is in opposition to it."

The Roman church felt that the disciples who received communion from Jesus at His Last Supper before he was crucified represented the clergy; therefore, only clergy should partake of both the bread and the wine in the Eucharist services. As a result, the clergy had been giving the people only the bread, contending that it represented Jesus' body, and the body contains both flesh as well as blood. They didn't allow the people to partake of the chalice of wine. They said that wine was too precious and expensive to waste on the common people.

Contrary to the position of the Roman church, Wyclif and Hus and his followers felt that the disciples represented lay people, since Jesus functioned as pastor to them. If that interpretation was correct, then lay people should be able to partake of both the bread and the wine. Master Jakoubek of Stribro had begun to give both emblems to the people, in keeping with his belief that Wyclif and Hus wanted the Bible to supercede the traditions of the church. Hus' followers began to use the common chalice as their symbol representing a return to the practices of the "primitive" church described in the Bible as contrasted with the traditions of the Roman church.

Hus' attorney, Jan Jesenic, supporting the position that the pope was not the supreme authority, argued that Peter was not the prince of the apostles. He contended that Peter had the same power as the other apostles, except that he had been assigned to Rome; therefore, he was not the first in succession of popes. If that was the case, then whomever Christ put in authority over the people should retain all power. If it was a secular authority, then in Bohemia that person was King Wenceslas.

Hus had written that the chief ruler of the church was not the pope, but Christ. He also insisted that the true church was not a building or institution, but comprised of all people throughout time who have believed in Jesus Christ as their Savior, and that their identity was known only by God; however, Hus wasn't calling for the abolition of the institutional church but for its reform.

The Eucharist is important because it is symbolic of God's plan for saving all mankind and how He did it through Jesus Christ. The Bible tells how God created a perfect earth, where God and man could have a personal relationship with one another. But when the first people sinned, they broke that relationship. God's plan for restoring that relationship required that blood be shed in payment for sin. That blood had to come from a perfect sacrifice. Over the centuries of history, mankind has tried to make payment for sin by shedding the blood of animals and by doing good works, but these actions did not satisfy God.

Because people were unable to provide the perfect sacrifice on their own, God came to earth in the form of a man, Jesus, to be that sacrifice. He was born of a virgin in a humble stable, led a sinless life, performed many miracles proving that He was sent from God, and then allowed Himself to be unjustly tried and executed, dying a cruel death on the cross. He was the perfect, unblemished sacrifice, taking our sins upon Himself and shedding His blood in payment for our sins.

The Eucharist bread symbolizes Jesus' body which was broken for us, and the wine represents the blood He shed in payment for our sins. It is taken by all believers to show the unity and brotherhood of all who believe that Jesus is the One sent by God to save us from hell and death. It is also a reminder that Jesus promised to return a second time to rule and reign on earth. He will take all who believe in Him back to heaven with Him to live forever.

But why was there so much disagreement over how the Eucharist was celebrated?

Because allowing only the clergy to drink from the chalice of wine was a tradition instituted by men within the Roman church, making it seem that church traditions superceded the Bible as God's final authority. Jan Hus, Wyclif, and others like them felt that the Bible was the final authority, and that the Roman church, through the decisions by fallible and sinful men in positions of authority within it, was deviating from that Word.

It was such men, feeling that their positions were threatened, who were so active in attempting to silence Hus and the voices of those like him by accusing them of heresy. They used Wyclif's writings as the basis for their accusations against Jan Hus, since Hus supported many of Wyclif's positions. Unfortunately, the text they were using was a translation from English into Czech by the German Master John Hubner. Some Czech Masters at the university in Prague held that Hubner, an opponent of Wyclif and jealous of Hus' authority, had deliberately falsified the text. Jan Hus made it plain that he opposed the wholesale condemnation of Wyclif's 45 statements of doctrine **only** on the grounds that they misrepresented Wyclif's true teaching.

There weren't other copies of Wyclif's writings that could be presented to the councilors for comparison since the Archbishop had ordered that all copies be delivered to him, and he burned them. In his preaching Hus named 7 out of the 45 articles of belief stated by Wyclif that he dared not condemn. He did not defend the majority of the 45 articles which were being attacked. Jan only attempted to defend those articles of Wyclif's that he felt were wholly orthodox.

The pope's legal board, the Curia, placed Hus under an order prohibiting him from preaching or teaching, and invited him to attend the Ecumenical Council in Constance, in southern Germany on what is now the border with Switzerland. Their stated purpose was to eradicate heresy from the western church, and they wanted to determine if Jan Hus was involved in heresy.

Emperor Sigismund of Hungary promised Jan safe passage to and from the Council. Jan believed him, but it was only a trick to get him out of Bohemia. Sigismund's betrayal was intended to gain him support from Rome in extending his power in Central Europe. A week after Jan arrived in Constance he was thrown into prison. Jan's supporters tried to get him out, but they weren't successful. Friends smuggled out letters, and Czech noblemen signed their names to numerous formal protests. These were all ignored.

Jan languished for several months in a terrible, dark, dank prison cell in a Dominican monastery on an island in Lake Constance. Located next to the latrines, his cell was filled with the awful stench of unhealthy gases emanating from the sewage. Only when pressure was brought to arrange a visit by the pope's physician was his life saved. He was relocated to a better cell so that he would survive long enough to appear before the Council.

Any compassion shown him was short-lived. At this time three different popes, one in Rome, one in Pisa, one somewhere in France had been appointed by different factions of the church. A task of the Council was to resolve which one would be the true pope. The pope from Rome was in Constance. He was deposed by the Council, so he gave the keys to Jan's cell to Sigismund and fled. Rather than free Jan, Sigismund locked him in another, bleaker cell, in a tower with no roof. He was overheard to say about Jan, "There is enough to condemn him. If he will not recant his error, let him be burned." It was clear that Jan had no one at the Council to defend him.

When the Council received the protests from the Czech noblemen, they supposedly invited 452 nobles to appear before them at a hearing. Inexplicably, none came. It is possible that the invitations were never sent. At least, they never arrived at their intended destinations.

Hus was refused an opportunity to defend his ideas or reply to specific charges. When he attempted to argue his case, he was shouted down. They asked him if he believed that Wyclif was in heaven or hell. He replied, "I, however, not wishing to pass temerous judgement, hope that he is of the number of the saved. If he is in heaven, may the glorious Lord who placed him there be praised; if he is in purgatory, may the merciful Lord free him quickly; if he is in hell, may he, in accordance with God's judgement, remain until eternal fulfillment."

The Council wanted either a clear condemnation of Wyclif or solid support of Wyclif's positions. Hus' responses to their questions seemed to be an effort to obscure his true position. Since he gave neither an approval or denial, the Council followed their initial inclination, which was to assume that Hus agreed with all Wyclif espoused.

Between hearings, Jan was allowed visits with some of the lords. They tried to convince him to compromise his beliefs. He told two of them, "I beseech you by the bowels of Christ to flee evil priests but love good ones according to their works, and, together with other faithful barons and lords, to the extent of your power, not to permit these good priests to be oppressed. It is indeed for this that God has set you over others. I believe that there will be a great persecution in the Kingdom of Bohemia of those who faithfully serve God, if God does not intervene through the secular lords, whom He has enlightened more than the spiritual ones in His Law." Jan refused to recant because he said that he never taught the errors ascribed to him.

At his final hearing, 30 charges were presented against him. Some were preposterous, including that he had taught that he was the fourth person of the Godhead! He rejected all charges, but his voice was drowned by the waves of derisive shouts. Unable to present a defense, Jan stood, chained and emaciated, before the assembled cardinals and bishops. Priestly garments were laid out on a table before him. The demand was then made for Jan to either recant or die.

At last he was permitted to speak. He said that to recant would mean to commit perjury, to lie. Instantly his voice was smothered by an explosion of venomous shouts, as the air filled with papers and other objects being thrown at him by the Council members. The cardinals and bishops were on their feet, shaking fists and threatening to break down the railings to get to Jan. Into the face of this violent word storm, Jan tried to tell them that their facts were wrong. He asked them to show him his errors from the Scriptures. Their rage overwhelmed all reason, and they sealed their ears to his entreaties.

His sentence was pronounced and it was **death!**

Jan dropped to his knees in prayer, crying out an appeal to God, but the Council leaders gnashed their teeth and spat that such an appeal was erroneous because it contradicted canon law. Silence fell on the hall as council members resumed their seats to relish the final humiliation of the accused. Jan, in resignation, squared his shoulders and looked his accusers in the eye, stating in a calm voice that he preferred to be burned in public than silenced in private, "...in order that all Christendom might know what I said in the end." As the jeers began again, he prayed aloud that Christ might forgive his judges and accusers. The jeering rose in volume.

Seven bishops stepped forward and draped Jan in priestly vestments, shoving his arms into the sleeves. As roughly as they had put them on, they then tore off each in turn, saying, "O cursed Judas...we take from you the cup of redemption," concluding with the words, "We commit your soul to the devil." They then crammed on his head a tall, conical paper hat upon which were painted three demons and the inscription, "This is a heretic".

The Council sat back in satisfaction, their "holy" work complete. Now it was up to the executioner to do his work. Like Pontius Pilate, the cardinals and bishops stood, mentally washed their hands of any blame in Hus' death, and solemnly filed out of the hall. Their guards pushed the "heretic" ahead of them through the streets to the place of death.

Jan was shoved against a stake planted in the town square and bound to it by a sooty chain wrapped around his neck. His body was crushed against the stake by bundles of sticks stacked up to his chin in a heavy pyramid of wood. Though he could barely breath from the weight of the fuel, he was given one last chance to recant. The crowd filling the square fell silent to hear his words.

Struggling to take a breath, Jan called out clearly, "God is my witness that...the principal intention of my preaching and of all my other acts or writings was solely that I might turn men from sin." He drew another deep breath and continued, "And in that truth of the Gospels that I wrote, taught, and preached in accordance with the sayings and expositions of the holy doctors, I am willing to die today."

The words had scarcely left Jan Hus' lips when one of the cardinals, turning his back on Jan in scorn, gave a casual wave of his hand as a signal to the executioner. The man hesitated a moment, eyes peering from the black hood shifting from Jan to the burning faggot in his hand. Then he sighed, shuffled forward and shoved the torch among the bundles of wood. There was a momentary crackling as the dry kindling inhaled the flames, then the pyre roared to life, a wall of heat forcing the executioner backwards. The crowd also, including priests, bishops and guards, pushed backwards against the throng away from the intensity of the blaze.

As the flames and smoke shot upward into Constance's still blue sky, Jan Hus' voice could be heard above the roar of burning wood. He sang, "Jesus, Son of the Living God, have mercy on me." He was heard singing these words three times, and then there was only the sound of the crackle and pop of the flames.

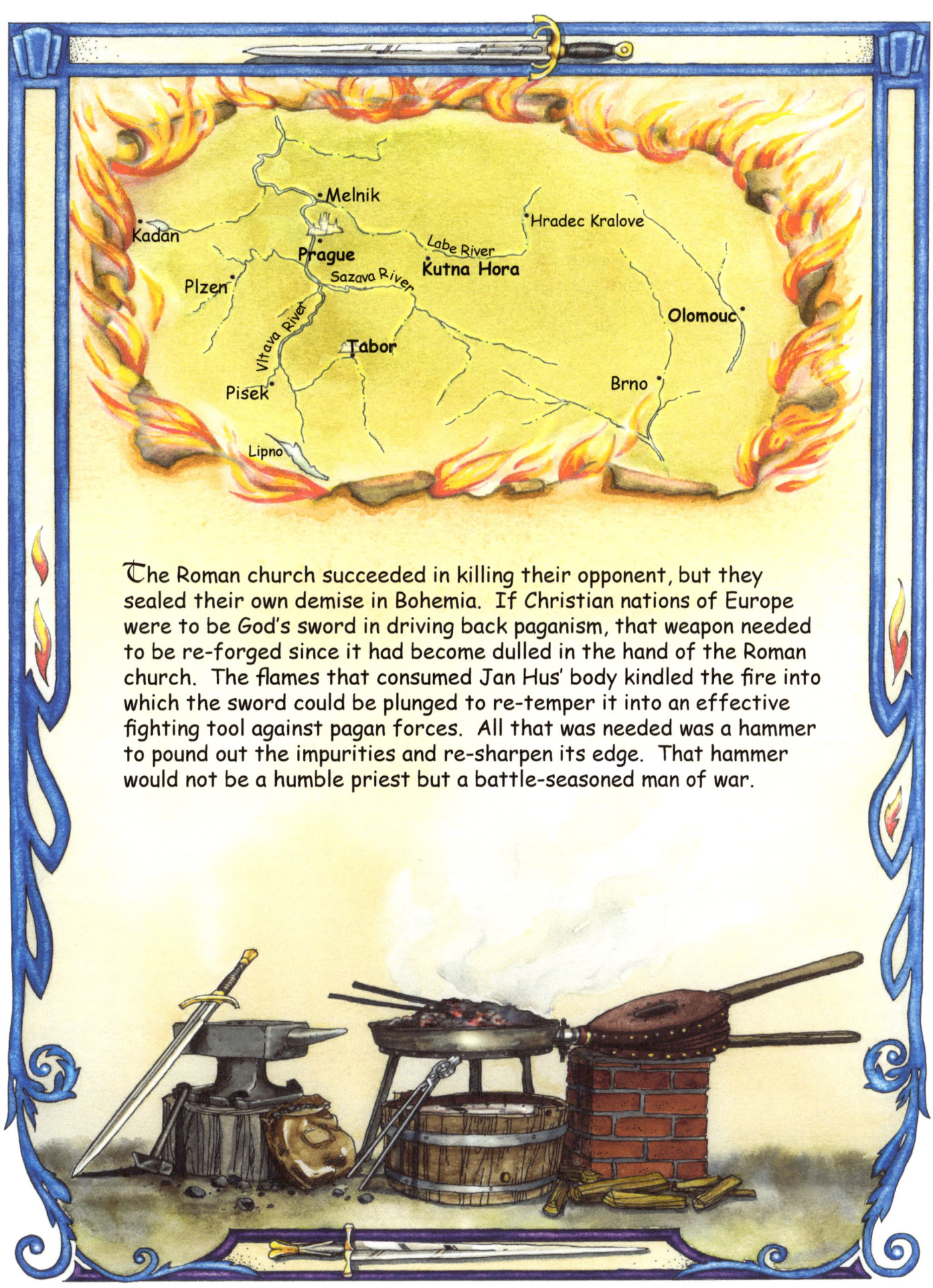

The Roman church succeeded in killing their opponent, but they sealed their own demise in Bohemia. If Christian nations of Europe were to be God's sword in driving back paganism, that weapon needed to be re-forged since it had become dulled in the hand of the Roman church. The flames that consumed Jan Hus' body kindled the fire into which the sword could be plunged to re-temper it into an effective fighting tool against pagan forces. All that was needed was a hammer to pound out the impurities and re-sharpen its edge. That hammer would not be a humble priest but a battle-seasoned man of war.

Part Two

JAN ZIZKA

Hammer of God

Jan Hus' execution sent shock waves through Bohemia. Nearly 500 Czech nobles gathered in Prague and entered into a solemn covenant, pledging to defend Hus' ideals against all external threats. Out of their gathering emerged a manifesto which would cause the people to choose whether to support Rome's position or that of the Czech reformers. The manifesto drawn up by the nobles was called, "The Four Articles of Prague". As an extension of Hus' basic philosophy, it stated:

1. The Word of God is to be preached freely;
2. The sacrament of the body and blood of Christ is to be served in the form of both bread and wine to all faithful Christians;
3. Priests are to relinquish earthly position and possessions, and all are to begin an obedient life based on the apostolic model; and
4. All public sins and public sinners in all positions are to be restrained.

These nobles agreed to appoint their own bishops and be submissive only to them.

Out of the gathering also emerged a determination to select a leader to defend Bohemia against an invasion by foreign troops. The leader would need to be brave beyond measure, hardened by battle, and skilled in the tactics of warfare.

The man they chose was Jan Zizka. He would lead the defenders of Jan Hus, known as Hussites, in battle. Born Jan of Trocznow, he had lost one eye early in life. Zizka is said to mean "one-eyed", but this disability didn't hinder him from becoming a great warrior and tactician. He had gained military experience in wars with the Poles and in fighting against the Muslim armies which were advancing through the passes of the Carpathian Mountains in Hungary. Jan had good reason to lead the Hussite forces against those who would try to enforce Rome's authority against Hus' true believers. He carried in his bosom the memory of a grievous wrong done his sister by a wicked priest, and he warmly espoused the views of Jan Hus. He shared a deep indignation at Hus' fate and was committed to avenging this great wrong.

Many German residents were mixed with the population in Moravia, the northeastern part of what is now the Czech Republic. These Germans resented what they saw as a Czech rebellion against the Roman church which they supported. On June 24, 1415, German residents in Olomouc, Moravia, burned to death two lay preachers of "Hus' errors". This enflamed those who believed in Hussite principles, and the battle lines were drawn. The Czech nobility and Hussites were on one side, and the German residents and Catholic townspeople on the other. Although not yet open war, it was a precursor. Citizens were taking sides within their towns, and skirmishes flared up throughout the countryside.

In Prague, the priests were divided into those who supported Rome and those who stood by Hus' principles. By September, Bishop Zelezny of the Roman faction had been appointed to enforce antiheresy principles against the Hussites, including the seizing of lands. For their part, all but three of the sixty-one Czech barons formed the "Hussite League", condemning the execution of Hus, and vowing to defend, to the point of shedding blood, the law of Christ. King Wenceslas watched to see which side was the strongest before deciding which to support.

Jan Zizka organized forces to protect the Hussites. He designated five villages to provide refuge for people driven from their homes by the Roman faction. For three years the two factions battled one another. Supporters of Rome drove Hussite priests out of towns and villages, and Hussites expelled Roman priests from towns, seizing their lands and smashing church images. Hus' supporters migrated to the towns of refuge, the major of which was Tabor, a self-governing city which became the center of the Hussite movement. Jan Zizka oversaw the building of its extensive fortifications, so that it was both a military stronghold and a place where a new form of worship services could be instituted.

By April, 1418, most of the German faculty at the Prague university had left, leaving the Czech faculty in the majority, so the university adopted the Hussite position. The balance of religious power had shifted away from the Roman church. This made the new pope in Rome fearful that Bohemia would be lost to Roman influence. Since King Wenceslas was not protecting Roman clergy, the pope authorized Sigismund, Emperor of Hungary, to proceed with armed action against the Hussites. It was, in fact, an order to invade Bohemia. The flames kindled by Jan Hus had now spread outside Bohemia to include the Hungarian Empire and Silesia's Germans, who would make up part of Sigismund's army.

Jan Zizka was intimately familiar with Silesia, part of present Poland. Earlier, he had led Czech forces alongside the Poles in defeating the "invincible" Teutonic Knights. The Knights, supposedly a Christian order, had ruled much of northern Europe for generations. Their tactics were anything but Christian. They had precipitated a crusade against Poland and Lithuania, persuading Rome and the crusading knights of Europe that their opponents were pagans. In fact, King Jagiello of Lithuania had been baptized and required that his people cut down their sacred groves, destroy all pagan idols, and convert to Christianity. The Knights' lies were intended to generate support for their attempt to conquer Lithuania and gain important Baltic Ports. Together with Poland, Jagiello stood against the Knights' territorial aims, and Zizka stood with Jagiello to protect against this affront to Christianity. At the Battle of Tannenberg, Zizka's key role and resolute courage were crucial to Jagiello's victory. His experience with the battle strategies and thought processes of the Polish generals gave him an advantage over Sigismund, particularly since Sigismund's Hungarians would rely heavily on their Silesian allies.

Sigismund was pleased that the pope had assigned him the task of intervening on Rome's behalf in Bohemia. By accepting the pope's assignment, he overestimated his own ability to quickly resolve the church's problem. He may also have been blinded by his desire to assume the throne of Bohemia as a spoil of war. Although he was intent on defending the church, his opponent, Jan Zizka, was intent on defending the Christian faith. This distinction would be the key to a God-given victory.

On July 30, 1419, word reached Prague that Sigismund's troops were gathered on the Bohemian border. The Roman faction in Prague quickly appointed new Catholic councilmen, hoping to tip the balance of power in favor of Rome and thus avoid war. To counter this move, congregants in churches throughout Prague came to church armed, and led by Jan Zizka and the preacher Jan Zelivsky, approached the city tower. Someone inside the tower dropped a stone which struck one of the Hussites. This blow began the war, and the Hussites responded by storming the city tower. They demanded the release of imprisoned reformers, and when they were refused, cast 13 of the new councilmen out of the windows to their deaths on the spears and lances below. Since King Wenceslas had fled Prague, the queen, who had remained behind, immediately appointed new magistrates favorable to the Hussite position.

The news of what had taken place in Prague threw King Wenceslas into a rage. As he poured forth a torrent of abuse, one of his attendants ventured to say that he had foreseen what had taken place. Wenceslas sprang upon the speaker, drawing his dagger. Had the attendants not forcibly restrained the king he would have murdered the man on the spot. Instead, the king's fit of passion led to his own death. He was struck with paralysis, and 18 days later had a second stroke and died. Like the death of King Herod in the Book of Acts, Chapter 12 in the Bible, Wenceslas' death showed that even rulers of mighty kingdoms are under God's hand and will suffer calamity if they oppose His will.

Since King Wenceslas had no children, Sigismund, Wenceslas' half-brother, was the likely successor to the throne. Word of the events in Prague were received by Sigismund as a welcomed omen. Now he could both carry out the pope's orders and assume the throne he coveted. He moved his non-Czech mainly anti-Hussite troops across the border to restore order and re-establish Roman rule of the church.

When the citizens of Prague learned that the queen had secretly been negotiating with the Germans, they flew to arms and called upon Zizka for aid. He appeared before the walls of the city with four thousand troops and drove the queen's garrison back into the castle. Terms were offered for a truce, and the Hussites were allowed to celebrate the Lord's Supper in their own way. The law of God and truth of the Gospel were permitted to be maintained throughout the kingdom. The queen fled from Prague in the dark of night, leaving Prague in the hands of Zizka and his army.

Sigismund's troops spread throughout the countryside, inflicting violence and insult on any supporters of the Hussites that they found. They imprisoned some, sold others as slaves and put many to death. Priests were tied to trees and burned alive. Sixteen hundred people died in the early stages of the invasion. Any hope Sigismund may have had of a rapid conquest were dashed when he found himself confronted by armies led by Jan Zizka and Nicholas of Hus. The Hussite soldiers may have been peasants, but they fought with unexpected ferocity. The prospect of Sigismund, the betrayer of Hus, ascending the throne of Bohemia served to unite the people in their determination to gain religious liberty. Sigismund was fighting for territory and personal gain, but the people were fighting for their lives and the right to worship God as they pleased.

Zizka had prepared for the confrontation by training and arming a militia. He had his troops turn farm implements such as studded threshing flails into weapons. Pikes were made from pruning hooks, and war-wagons created. These armored peasant wagons could be chained together to create a mobile fortress wall from which firearms would be used for the first time in Europe as a major weapon in warfare. Zizka armed the wagons with mortars and men carrying hand-held cannons. The war-wagons were so formidable that many times the enemy would flee when they heard the wagons approaching.

Zizka encouraged his troops, "May God grant, dear brethren, that, performing good works, like the true children of your heavenly Father, you may remain steadfast in His fear! Let not affliction abate your courage; imitate the old Bohemians, your ancestors, always ready to defend God's cause and their own. Let us constantly have before our eyes the divine law and the common good, and let whoever knows how to handle a knife, or to throw a stone, or to brandish a club, be ready to march...The hand of God is not shortened; courage, therefore, and be ready."

Sigismund discovered that he was facing a formidable enemy, wholly committed to the fight. His troops, though fully armored and armed, were driven back time and again, crushed by Zizka's armed peasants. The heavy, studded flails and pruning hooks in the hands of people trusting in God's protection and willing to die for the cause of Christ were proving more than a match for swords and lances. After each victory Zizka's troops were able to re-arm themselves with the weaponry discarded on the field by Sigismund's dead or defeated soldiers, thereby growing stronger and stronger.

War raged throughout the land, and the royalists under Sigismund, frustrated at not achieving an easy victory, adopted a strategy of terror. They captured Kutna Hora in northern Bohemia and established an extermination center. Hundreds of captured Hussites were taken there and thrown down mineshafts to their deaths. By March 1420, the pope recognized that stronger measures had to be taken or Zizka's forces, which were hammer-

ing the fight out of Sigismund's army, might prevail. He authorized Sigismund to exterminate all Wyclifites, Hussites and other "heretics". The conflict was now more than just a war; it was a crusade against these Christians whose "heresy" was a belief in communion using both elements, an apostolic lifestyle for the clergy, and a moral lifestyle for all. Instead of re-energizing Sigismund's forces, the pope's order caused every Czech to feel obliged to fight off the essentially German invaders. The fighting intensified from town to town, and even Prague was occupied by each side in turn.

Throughout Europe other rulers were watching the outcome of the conflict in Bohemia. When Zizka's forces were about to defeat Sigismund, Prince Sigmund Korybut of Poland/Lithuania decided to send an army to reinforce the Roman side. He crossed into Moravia and Bohemia from the north, and on May 17, 1422, his forces entered Prague, restoring order and turning it back to those masters and barons who supported the Roman Church.

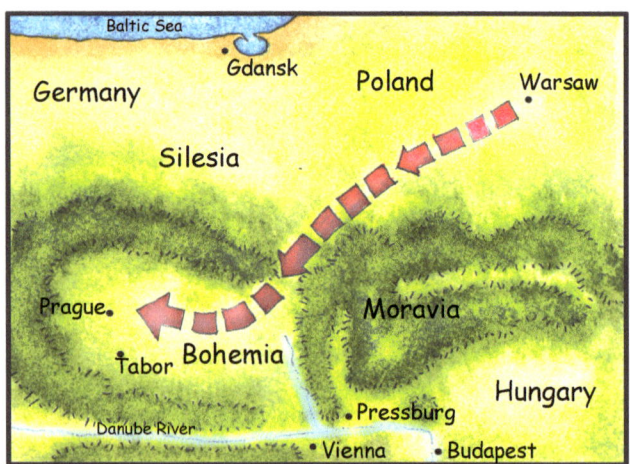

Jan Zizka, although having begun the war with one eye and having lost his second one in battle, continued to fight. With mace in hand, he led his troops against the coalition of Catholic and Prague barons, defeating them time and again, and never losing a battle. The head of that mace, Zizka's symbol, was a fist holding a dagger. The sight of him in the midst of a melee, eyes bandaged and armed with just that weapon, inspired his troops to remarkable feats of valor. Having decimated Sigismund's forces in battle after battle and having achieved a decisive victory at the key strategic town of Malesov, he turned his army of Christian peasants toward Prague. There, with an army exhausted from four years of constant war, and with many wounded from the terrible fighting at Malesov, Zizka was confronted by Prince Sigmund Korybut's fresh army. It was time to negotiate an end to the conflict, and in September, he made peace.

Jan Zizka's own body was battered and scarred, like the land he had defended. He had succeeded in hammering the common people into a fighting force that, like a sharpened sword, had severed the corruption of the Roman Church from the true believers of Bohemia. He had shown that, with God's help, it is possible for those who believe in the simple truth of the Bible to prevail over the might of the largest armies that can be sent against a nation. And he had shown Europe that the time had come for all those who believe in God to return to the teachings of Christ, free from the additions of corrupt men.

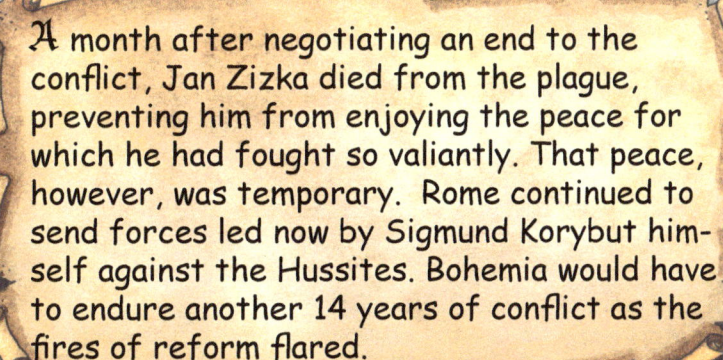

A month after negotiating an end to the conflict, Jan Zizka died from the plague, preventing him from enjoying the peace for which he had fought so valiantly. That peace, however, was temporary. Rome continued to send forces led now by Sigmund Korybut himself against the Hussites. Bohemia would have to endure another 14 years of conflict as the fires of reform flared.

Does that mean that all Jan Hus and Jan Zizka and their supporters did was for nothing?

No, not at all. What they did had a tremendous impact on living conditions for people not only in Bohemia and Moravia, but for all of Europe.

The followers of Jan Hus, by forming a self-governing city-state at Tabor, achieved the education of both men and women, teaching all to read the Bible for themselves. This was unheard of in most of Europe at that time. The result of this labor would be the spread of knowledge of God's Word to the common people, preparing the soil of Europe for the coming Reformation - a return to believing that the Bible is God's highest authority.

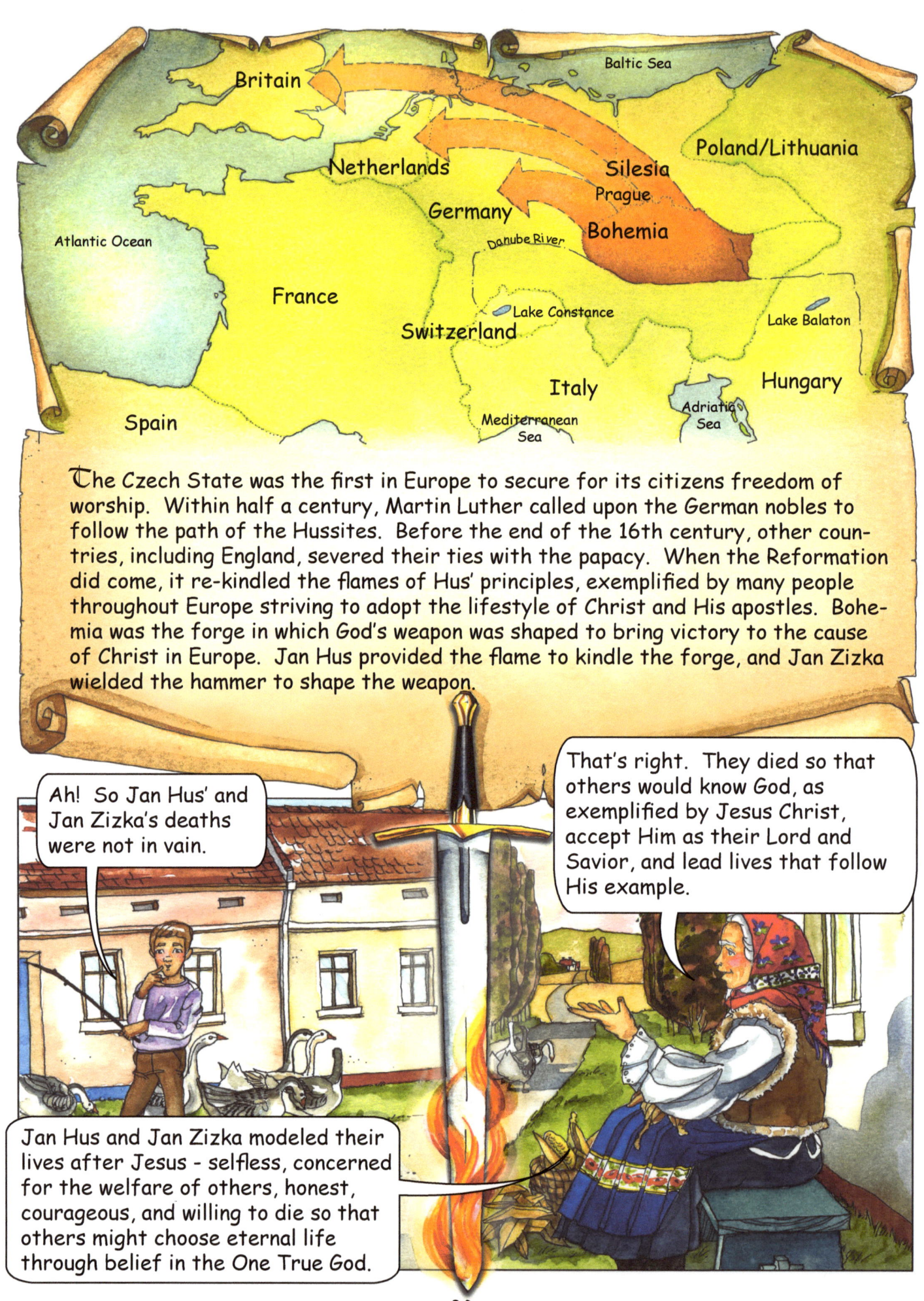

Bibliography

Aid Camps International, *Jan Zizka*, Mark us http://www.free-template.org/./ja/Janzizka.html.

Bartos, Frantisek Michalek, *The Hussite Revolution 1424-1437*, Klassen, John, ed., East European Monographs, Boulder, N.Y., N.Y.: Columbia University Press, 1986.

"Blind Courage, The Unique Genius of Jan Zizka", www.snowcrest.net/ggriff/index..., from *The Very Pretty Chronicles of Jan Zizka*.

Davies, Norman, *God's Playground, A History of Poland*, Vol. I, N.Y., N.Y.: Columbia University Press, 2005.

Eliade, Mircia, *The Encyclopedia of Religion*, N.Y., N.Y.: MacMillan Publishing Co., 1987, pp. 535-536.

Gerrish, Chris, *Jan Hus*, http:/www.patricia gray.net/Musichtmis/Papers120/Hus.html.

Heymann, Frederick G., *Poland and Czechoslovakia*, Englewood Cliffs, N.J.: Prentiss-Hall, Inc., 1966, pp. 21-75.

"History, Christian", Issue 68, Vol. XIX, No. 4, *Christianity Today, Inc.*, Carol Stream, IL., Jan., 2004

Kaminsky, Howard, *A History of the Hussite Revolution*, Berkeley, CA.: University of California Press, 1967.

Lendvai, Paul, *The Hungarians*, Princeton, N.J.: Princeton University Press, 1999.

Lukowski, Jerzy and Hubert Zawadzki, *A Concise History of Poland*, Cambridge, UK.: Cambridge University Press, 2001.

McManners, John, *The Oxford Illustrated History of Christianity*, Oxford, N.Y.: Oxford University Press, 1990, pp. 99-121.

Mears, John W., D.D., *Heroes of Bohemia: Huss, Jerome and Zisca*, Philadelphia: Westcott and Thomson, 1879.

Murray, Albert V., *Crusade and Conversion On The Baltic Frontier 1150-1500*, Hampshire, England,: Ashgate Publishing Limited, 2001.

Newark, Tim, *Medieval Warlords*, Dorset, England,: Blandford Press, 1987.

Odlozilik, Otakar, *The Hussite King, Bohemia In European Affairs 1440-1471*, New Brunswick, N.J.: Rutgers University Press, 1965, pp. 3-18.

Rabb, Theodore K., *Renaissance Lives, Portraits of an Age*, N.Y., N.Y.: Pantheon Books, 1993.

Racinet, Albert, *Weltgeschichte Der Kostume*, Koln,: Parkland Verlag, 1995.

Roubiczek, Paul and Joseph Kalmer, *Warrior of God, The Life and Death of Jan Hus*, London,: Nicholson and Watson, 1947.

Sarnowsky, Jurgen, *Mendicants, Military Orders, and Regionalism in Medieval Europe*, England,: Ashgate Publishing Limited, 1999.

"Slavic Unity", Slavija, *The Battle of Grunwald*, http://nationalism.org/slavic/21060201.html.

Spinka, Matthew, *Jan Hus a Biography*, Princeton, N.J.: Princeton University Press, 1968.

Spinka, Matthew, *Jan Hus and the Czech Reform*, Hamden, CT.: Archon Books, 1966.

Turnbull, Stephen, *Tannenberg 1410, Disaster for the Teutonic Knights*, N.Y., N.Y.: Osprey Publishing, 2003.

Vischer, Melchior, *Jan Hus, Au Fruhr Wider Papst und Reich*, Frankfurt A, Mein.:Societats-Verlag, 1955.

Ziegler, Uwe, *Kreuz und Schwert, De Geschichte des Deutschen Ordenz*, Koln, Bohlau Verlag, 2003.

About the Authors

Jerry and Faith McCollough are Assemblies of God missionaries and Gospel illustrators. They were trained as commercial artists at Woodbury University in Los Angeles, California, and began working together on illustrations while serving in Brussels, Belgium. Their interest in writing historical books about Christian heroes began while working with students in Bulgaria and developed during the years they lived in the former Czechoslovakia.

Research on their first book about the lives of Cyril and Methodius, the brothers who created the Cyrillic alphabet led them to discover other Christan heroes whose lives had a strong impact on the culture of Europe. Interest in history, archaeology, and the study of the development of Christianity throughout the world has taken them to 28 countries where they have been able to gather first hand knowledge of the sites and architecture of the locations they illustrate.

Jerry and Faith work together on the research, writing and production. Jerry does the black and white illustrations with a technical pen on illustration board. Faith does the color work in watercolor directly on the illustrations. She then does the prepress work including typesetting on the computer.

They both have a Bachelor's Degree in Commerical Art and Jerry has a Master's Degree in Biblical Literature. They have two children and four grandchildren.

Tell The Kids...

Jan Hus and Jan Zhizhka and the people of Bohemia wanted to celebrate the love of God, and the blessings He poured out on them through the life and sacrifice of Jesus, His son. They knew that prior to Jesus' coming to earth there was always the fear of death, but He took all their sins on Himself by His sacrificial death on the cross, on their behalf. Then, after three days He arose from the dead and walked among the people before ascending into heaven in front of a multitude. This showed them that death is no longer fearful for those who believe in Jesus and accept God's teaching through Him.

The Bohemians wanted to recognize Jesus' sacrifice on their behalf by taking both emblems of His death – the bread representing His broken body, and the wine representing His shed blood – in their celebration of the Lord's Supper, and they were willing to give their lives for that privilege.

-Do you, too, believe that God sent Jesus into the world to reveal God to us, and to give His life on the cross, taking your sins upon Himself so that you, too, can have eternal life?

-Are you willing to make Jesus Lord of your life, reading the Bible and following His teachings?

-If so, then tell God. You can do this very simply by praying the following: "Jesus, I acknowledge that you are God's Son, I accept you as my Savior and Lord. I ask you to forgive me of my sins. Please come into my heart and guide me in the way I should go."

That's all there is to it.

Now, find a Bible, and try to read it every day, to help you know God, and how He wants you to live. Remember that you can talk to God whenever you want, that is called praying. He speaks to you as you read the Bible, and the Holy Spirit will help you understand what it says.

Find a church where God's Word is taught, and where there are other believers who can provide fellowship, guidance, and support as you walk in life as a new person, blest of God, and blessing others. God loves you and wants you to make Him part of your life.... And tell others about Jesus, and how their lives, also, can be changed!!!

- Jerry McCollough

www.ingramcontent.com/pod-product-compliance
Lightning Source LLC
Chambersburg PA
CBHW041101070526
44579CB00003B/33